Especially for

Pat

From

Glenda Lawson

Date

12/21/2013

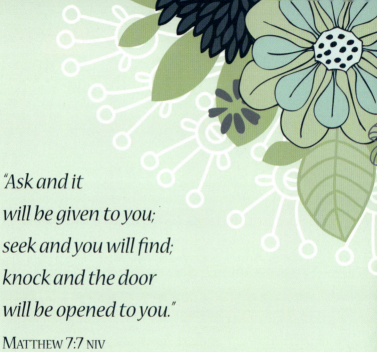

*"Ask and it
will be given to you;
seek and you will find;
knock and the door
will be opened to you."*

Matthew 7:7 NIV

© 2011 by Barbour Publishing, Inc.

ISBN 978-1-61626-313-3

Written and compiled by Pamela McQuade.

All rights reserved. No part of this publication may be reproduced or transmitted for commercial purposes, except for brief quotations in printed reviews, without written permission of the publisher.

Scripture quotations marked NIV are taken from the HOLY BIBLE, NEW INTERNATIONAL VERSION®. NIV®. Copyright © 1973, 1978, 1984, 2010 by Biblica, Inc.™. Used by permission. All rights reserved worldwide.

Scripture quotations marked ESV are from The Holy Bible, English Standard Version®, copyright © 2001 by Crossway Bibles, a publishing ministry of Good News Publishers. Used by permission. All rights reserved.

Published by Barbour Publishing, Inc., P.O. Box 719, Uhrichsville, Ohio 44683, www.barbourbooks.com

Our mission is to publish and distribute inspirational products offering exceptional value and biblical encouragement to the masses.

Printed in China.

The secret of contentment is the realization that life is a gift, not a right.

ANONYMOUS

Just Breathe

BARBOUR

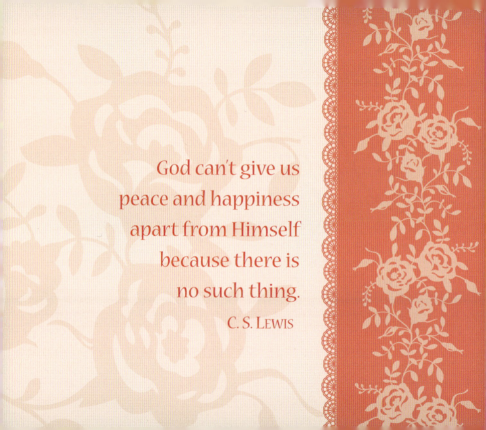

> God can't give us peace and happiness apart from Himself because there is no such thing.
>
> C. S. LEWIS

The best things in life are nearest:
breath in your nostrils,
light in your eyes,
flowers at your feet,
duties at your hand,
the path of right
just before you.
Robert Louis Stevenson

He that can take rest is greater than he that can take cities.

BENJAMIN FRANKLIN

Just breathe, and let
God's Spirit fill your soul.
In Him, your every
moment's in control.

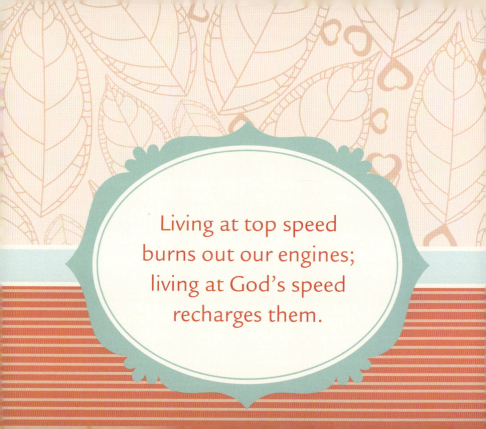

Living at top speed burns out our engines; living at God's speed recharges them.

To be of a peaceable spirit brings peace along with it.

THOMAS WATSON

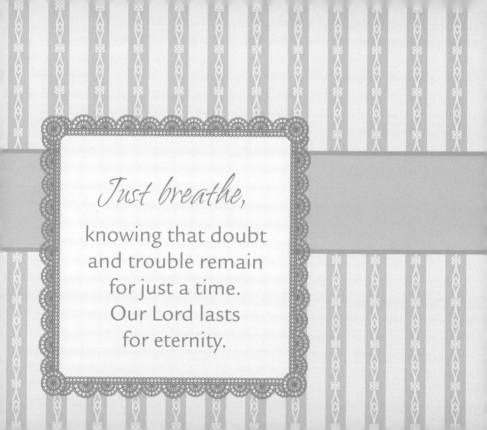

I learned what is obvious to a child.
That life is simply a collection of little lives,
each lived one day at a time.

NICHOLAS SPARKS

> Put off thy cares with thy clothes; so shall thy rest strengthen thy labor, and so thy labor sweeten thy rest.
>
> — Francis Quarles

The time to relax is— when you don't have time for it.

Sydney J. Harris

Just breathe in the joy
of knowing Jesus
and the security that
He loves you best.

There is only one basis
for really enjoying life,
and that is, to walk in
the way in which
God leads you.

LEAVES OF GOLD

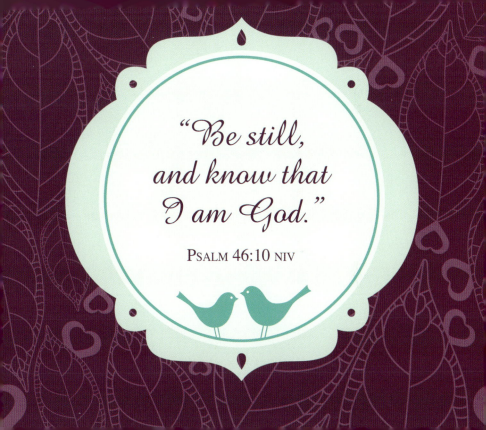

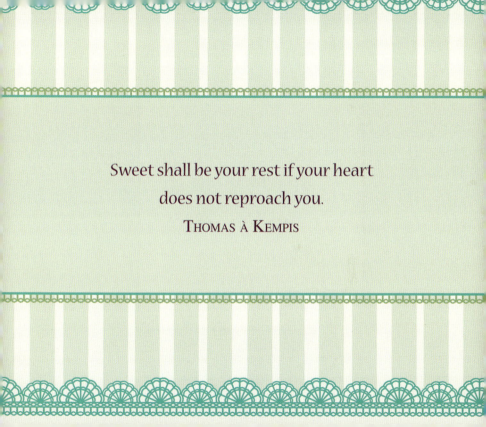

Sweet shall be your rest if your heart does not reproach you.

THOMAS À KEMPIS

The mind governed by the Spirit is life and peace.

ROMANS 8:6 NIV

God promises a safe landing but not a calm passage.

BULGARIAN PROVERB

He that lives in hope dances without music.

GEORGE HERBERT

The life of inner peace, being harmonious and without stress, is the easiest type of existence.

NORMAN VINCENT PEALE

My heart, which is so full to overflowing, has often been solaced and refreshed by music when sick and weary.

MARTIN LUTHER

For fast-acting relief, try slowing down.

LILY TOMLIN

Trust fully in God, and relaxation is always possible. Habitually thrust each care into His arms, and worry cannot overwhelm your life.

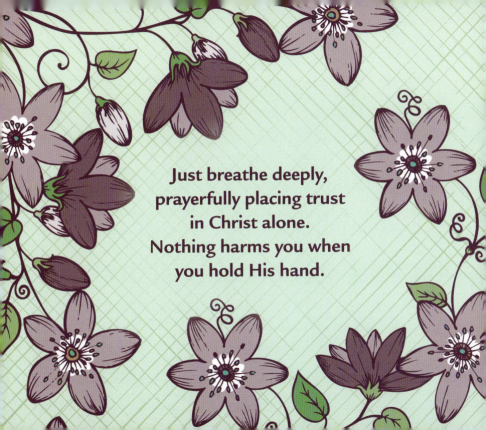

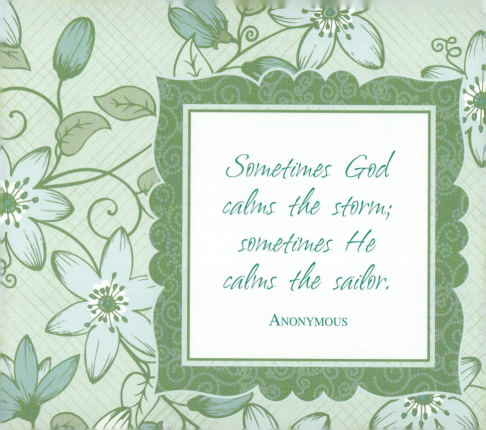

If a man. . .never allowed himself a bit of fun and relaxation, he would go mad or become unstable without knowing it.

HERODOTUS

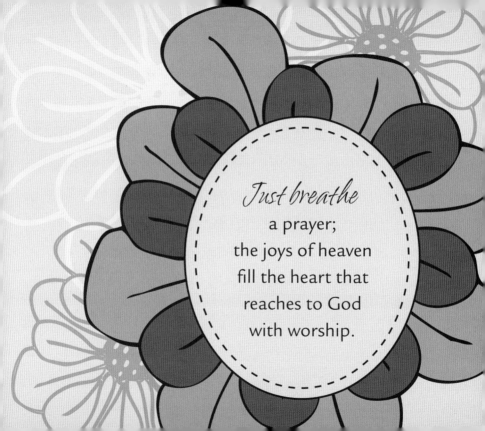

Seeing our Father
in everything
makes life
one long
thanksgiving
and gives rest
to the heart.

HANNAH WHITALL SMITH

Our thoughts,
not our feelings,
may lead us into tension.
Tame those thoughts,
and we tame our anxiety, too.

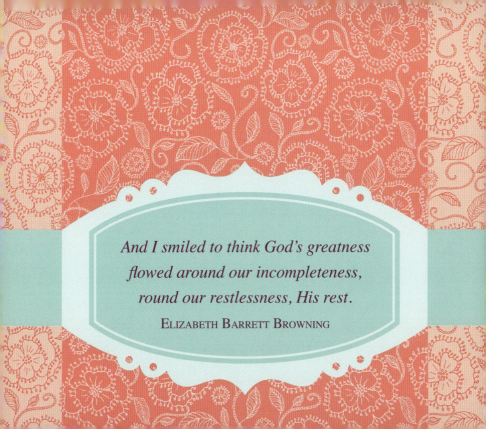

*And I smiled to think God's greatness
flowed around our incompleteness,
round our restlessness, His rest.*

ELIZABETH BARRETT BROWNING

Rest is the sweet sauce of labor.

PLUTARCH

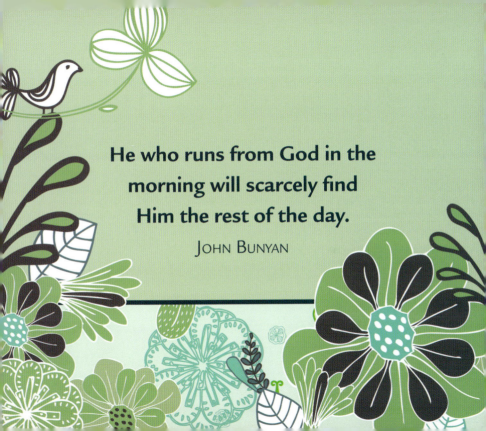

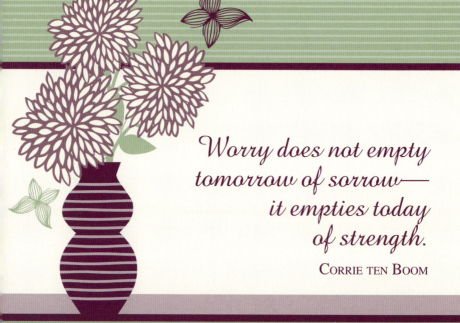

Worry does not empty tomorrow of sorrow—it empties today of strength.

CORRIE TEN BOOM

Worry is a useless mulling over of things we cannot change.

PEACE PILGRIM (MILDRED LISETTE NORMAN)

God's promises are like the stars;
the darker the night, the brighter they shine.

DAVID NICHOLAS

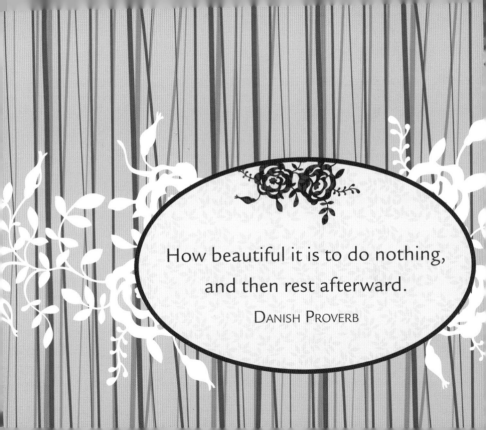

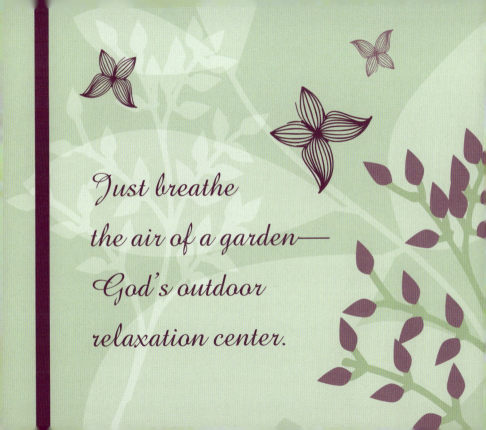

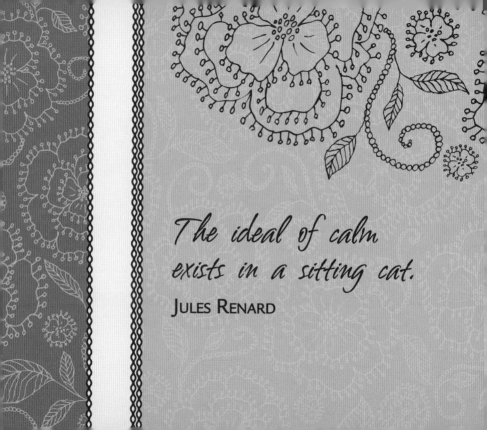

The ideal of calm exists in a sitting cat.

JULES RENARD

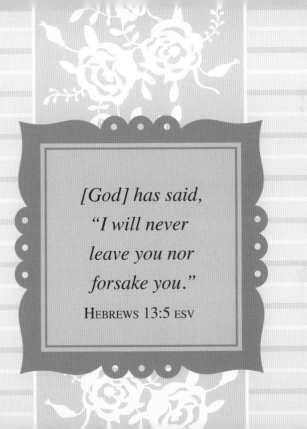

[God] has said, "I will never leave you nor forsake you."

HEBREWS 13:5 ESV

Our lives are not always simple, but when we trust God, they will always be blessed.

If people concentrated on the really important things in life, there'd be a shortage of fishing poles.

DOUG LARSON

People are just as happy as they make up their minds to be.

ABRAHAM LINCOLN

Nothing in this world is more relaxing than to lie down with a purring cat beside you.

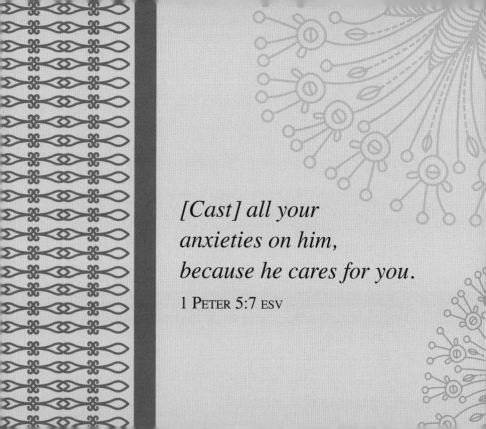

[Cast] all your anxieties on him, because he cares for you.

1 Peter 5:7 ESV

Good humor...lightens human burdens. It is the direct route to serenity and contentment.
GRENVILLE KLEISSER

Just breathe, when you have completed a task well. If you seek to do your best for Him, perfect performance need never become an idol.

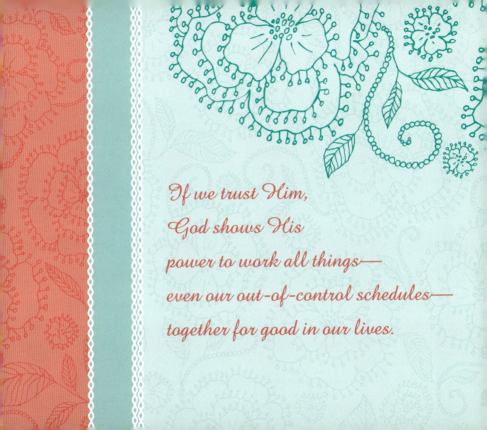

If we trust Him,
God shows His
power to work all things—
even our out-of-control schedules—
together for good in our lives.

Humor is a whisper from the soul, imploring mind and body to relax, let go, and be at peace again.

ANONYMOUS

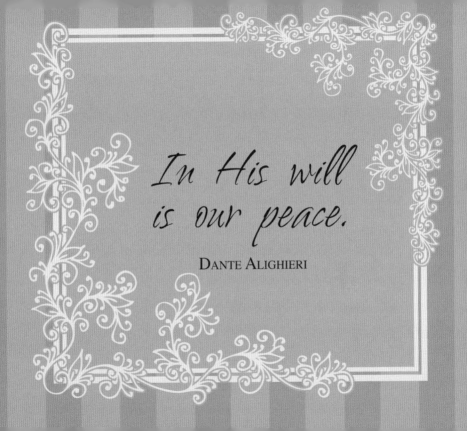

We delight in the beauty of the butterfly, but rarely admit the changes it has gone through to achieve that beauty.

MAYA ANGELOU

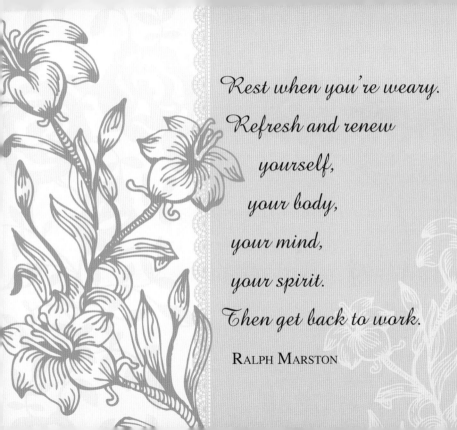

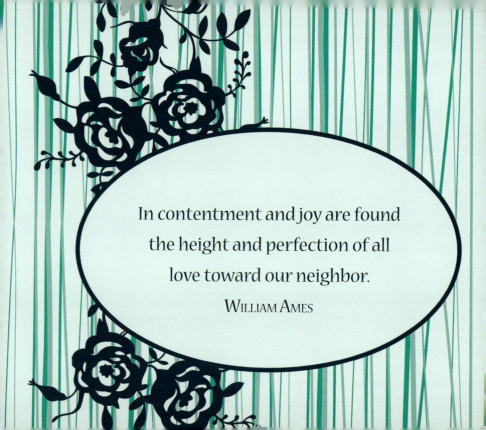

In contentment and joy are found the height and perfection of all love toward our neighbor.

WILLIAM AMES

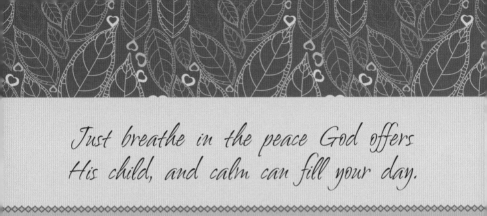

Just breathe in the peace God offers His child, and calm can fill your day.

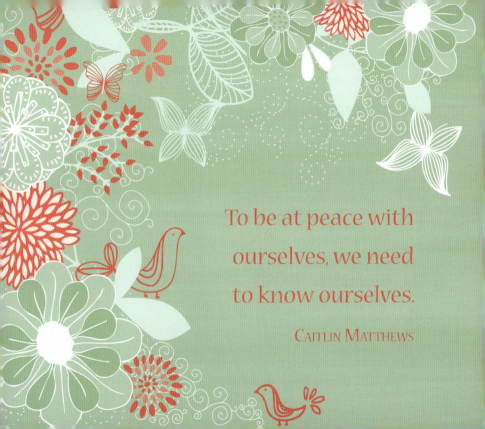

To be at peace with ourselves, we need to know ourselves.

CAITLIN MATTHEWS

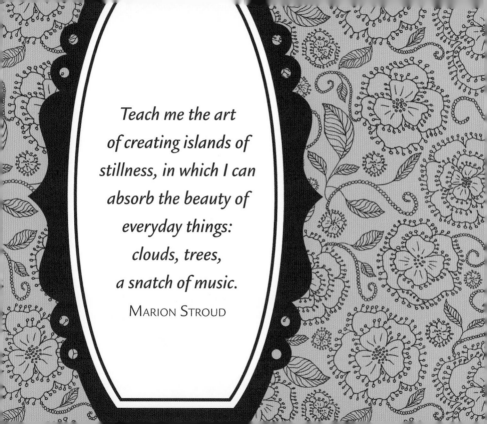

Teach me the art of creating islands of stillness, in which I can absorb the beauty of everyday things: clouds, trees, a snatch of music.

MARION STROUD

*Do not anticipate trouble,
or worry about what may never happen.
Keep in the sunlight.*

BENJAMIN FRANKLIN

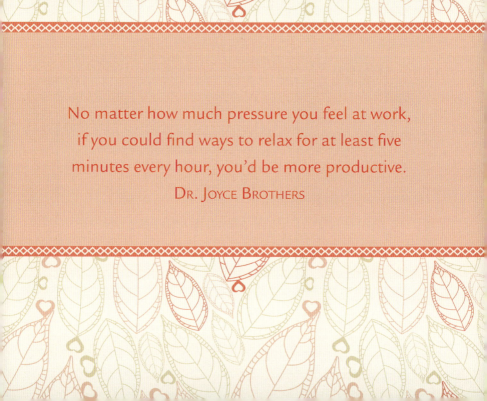

No matter how much pressure you feel at work, if you could find ways to relax for at least five minutes every hour, you'd be more productive.

Dr. Joyce Brothers

"Come to me, all you who are weary and burdened, and I will give you rest."

MATTHEW 11:28 NIV

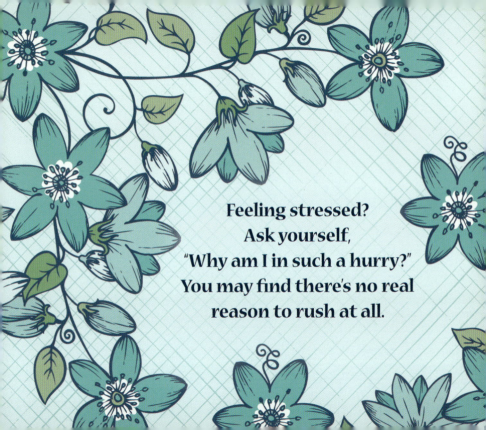

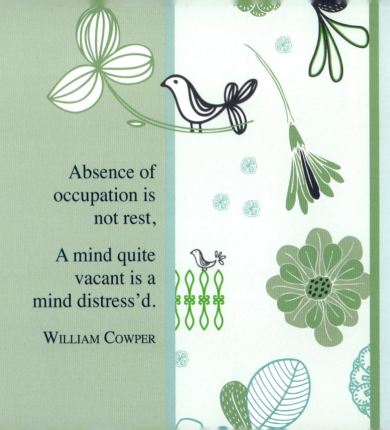

Absence of occupation is not rest,

A mind quite vacant is a mind distress'd.

WILLIAM COWPER

"You keep him in perfect peace whose mind is stayed on you, because he trusts in you."

ISAIAH 26:3 ESV

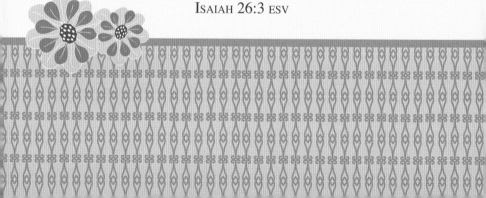

Thoughts filled with Jesus leave no room for despair.

Just breathe,
  as you walk the dog,
  delight in summer showers,
  or steep a warm cup of tea.
Small things help the mind relax.

> Sweet are the thoughts
> that savor of content.
> The quiet mind is
> richer than a crown.
>
> — Robert Greene

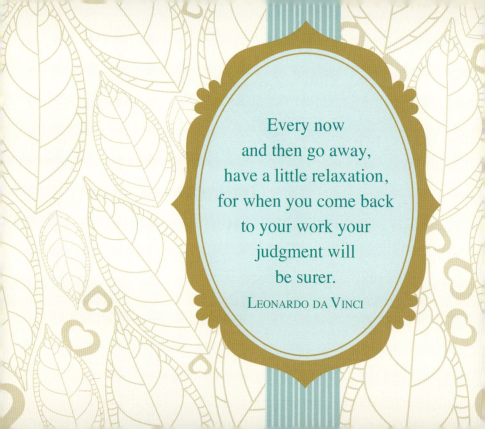

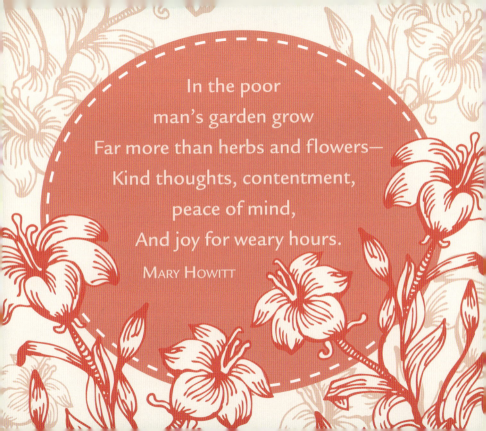

Stuck in traffic and stressed?
Relax, God will get you there.
Just slow down and let Him take control—
you can't change the situation anyway!

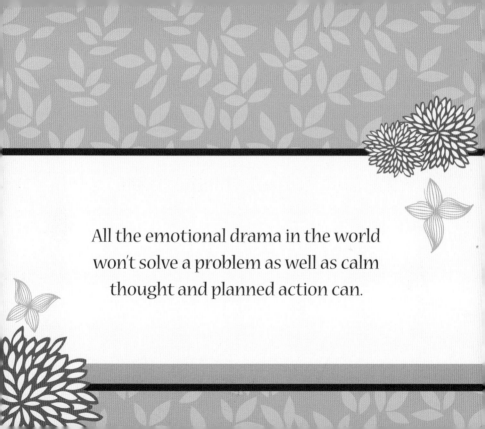

All the emotional drama in the world won't solve a problem as well as calm thought and planned action can.

Trouble and perplexity drive me to prayer, and prayer drives away perplexity and trouble.

Philip Melanchton